Approaching
GOD

Lessons from the Inspired Prayers of Scripture

BY LEE BRASE

NAVPRESS

Bringing Truth to Life

A *Pray!* Magazine book
Pray! Books • P.O. Box 35004, Colorado Springs, CO 80935
www.praymag.com

OUR GUARANTEE TO YOU

We believe so strongly in the message of our books that we are making this quality guarantee to you. If for any reason you are disappointed with the content of this book, return the title page to us with your name and address and we will refund to you the list price of the book. To help us serve you better, please briefly describe why you were disappointed. Mail your refund request to: NavPress, P.O. Box 35002, Colorado Springs, CO 80935.

Table of Contents

Introduction

Years ago it became evident to me that God wanted to develop my prayer life. I wasn't certain how this was to happen. As I prayed and thought about it, Luke 11:1 came to my attention. The disciples of Jesus wanted their prayer lives developed, so they asked Jesus, "Lord, teach us to pray." What struck me was Jesus' response to their request. He prayed! He did not teach them the theology or principles of prayer. He gave them an example to follow.

In the Bible God has recorded for us scores of sample prayers. He knew what kind of help we would need. These prayers in the Bible teach us how to converse with God in times of grief, stress, gratefulness, pain, frustration, warfare, joy, inner needs, danger, and uncertainty. There are psalms of praise and psalms of anger. There are prayers where people can only groan and prayers where people are articulate in their expressions. There are very specific requests and there are vague expressions of trusting God to work out His will.

The Language of Prayer

It helps to know that prayer is a language. It is a heart language. Children know how to learn a language. They learn to talk by first listening to others talk. They mimic the sounds they hear. At first children simply repeat the words of others, but eventually they express their own thoughts in their own words. They become fluent in their mother tongue and never forget it.

Jesus wanted the disciples to learn to talk to God with the language of the heart. He wanted prayer to become their mother tongue—their first language. He wanted them to eventually express their own thoughts in their own words. Desiring this, Jesus gave them a prayer that they could mimic (Lk. 11:1-4).

Because Jesus taught by example, I began looking for good models who could mentor me in prayer. Soon I discovered that some of the best models were in the Bible. When I saw this, I made a clear commitment to God to allow the praying people of the Bible to be my primary mentors in prayer.

For two decades I have been mentored by such people as Jesus, Paul, Moses, and David. As I meditated on their prayers I kept asking questions such as: Why did they pray? How did they approach God? What did they say to Him? What did they believe about God that made them pray the way they did? This last question was key because the most important factor in their prayer life was who they believed God to be.

Although their circumstances may have been different than ours, their prayers are still relevant. The purpose of this book is to allow the praying people of the Bible to mentor you in prayer. Let me introduce your prayer mentors:

- Nehemiah
- Paul
- Jeremiah
- the early disciples,
- David
- a tax collector
- Solomon
- Epaphras
- Hannah
- Isaac
- Jesus
- Moses

Have a wonderful adventure with them!

"Eternal God, it was You who created communications. You know more about this subject than humans will ever discover. Thank You for not only making us capable of communicating with You, but also for giving us the Bible to teach us to pray. Now I ask that You will cause the prayers in the Bible to come alive for those who read this book. Mentor them as only You can do. May great joy be brought to Your heart as Your children learn the language of their heart."

How to Use This Study

This study has been uniquely designed to allow you to be discipled directly by the pray-ers of the Bible. After a brief introduction to the mentor you will be working with, each chapter requires that you interact with Scripture and a series of questions first before you come to any commentary by the author.

Approach the Scripture and question portion with eyes and ears open. Ask the Holy Spirit to guide you into truth. Expect to be mentored by the prayers God recorded for all eternity.

After you have completed the question section of each chapter, the author provides further insights to each prayer portion. Each of the mentors in this book has been selected because of the unique approach he or she made toward God. Much can be learned by that interaction.

Once you have gone through the questions and commentary, there is space provided for you to *practice* what you've just learned through personal application. Don't skip this part! You are encouraged to take time to journal your prayer to God following your mentor's lead.

Be blessed as you journey through these pages!

Chapter One

Learning from Nehemiah

The Direct Approach

Nehemiah was an exiled Jew whose prayers propelled him into favor with his employer, Artaxerxes, King of Persia. His position of trust as the royal cupbearer earned him a voice with the king whose heart was moved to allow him to return to Jerusalem to rebuild. Imagine being in such a position. A hostage in a foreign country faced with the agonizing news that your beloved homeland has been destroyed . . . *how would you pray?*

Read Nehemiah 1:1-4.
How would you describe Nehemiah's mental state when he heard the news about Jerusalem?

What preparations did he make before making his specific request to God?

Read Nehemiah's prayer in verses 5-11.
How did Nehemiah's beliefs about God affect his prayer?

How did he address God in verse 5?

Nehemiah did not pray for the wall to be restored. Instead, his prayer consisted of three specific elements:

What did Nehemiah confess?

What did Nehemiah remind God of?

What did Nehemiah ask God to do?

Read Nehemiah 2:1-8.
Did the king's response to Nehemiah's request surprise you? Why or why not?

How was God addressed in these other prayers in the Bible? What were the pray-ers expecting God to do in response to their prayers?

2 Chronicles 6:14

Psalm 88:1

Daniel 9:4

A Closer Look

Several years ago, while my wife and I were living in a foreign country, we received word of my father's death. At the time, we had no way of returning to the United States. Feeling isolated and cut off from family, we grieved the loss of a loved one from a distance.

Nehemiah also lived in a foreign country and had little hope of ever returning home. Like most Jews, he loved his homeland. When one of the "brothers" came to Babylon, Nehemiah was full of questions about those back home and the beloved city of Jerusalem. What he heard left him in deep grief. For the next four months, his life was consumed with weeping, mourning, fasting, and praying. The Lord has kept a summary of this desperate man's prayers in Nehemiah 1:5-11:

> O LORD, God of heaven, the great and awesome God, who keeps
> his covenant of love with those who love him and obey his com-
> mands, let your ear be attentive and your eyes open to hear the
> prayer your servant is praying before you day and night for your ser-
> vants, the people of Israel. I confess the sins we Israelites, including

myself and my father's house, have committed against you. We have
acted very wickedly toward you. We have not obeyed the commands,
decrees and laws you gave your servant Moses.

Remember the instruction you gave your servant Moses, saying,
"If you are unfaithful, I will scatter you among the nations, but if
you return to me and obey my commands, then even if your exiled
people are at the farthest horizon, I will gather them from there and
bring them to the place I have chosen as a dwelling for my Name."

They are your servants and your people, whom you redeemed
by your great strength and your mighty hand. O Lord, let your ear
be attentive to the prayer of this your servant and to the prayer of
your servants who delight in revering your name. Give your servant
success today by granting him favor in the presence of this man.

Nehemiah intentionally called upon the "God, who keeps his covenant of love," and was no doubt aware of the tradition and heritage of this address. He had read this description in the writings of Moses (Dt. 7:9). He knew that Solomon, in his prayer dedicating the temple (2 Chron. 6:14), had referred to the Lord in this manner. And when Daniel pleaded for God to end Israel's captivity, he did so on the basis of the Lord being a covenant-keeping God (Dan. 9:4). Nehemiah longed to see God fulfill one of His great promises, so he naturally spoke to Him as one who keeps contact with His people.

Nehemiah's prayer is a good example of addressing God in a way that's consistent with what and how we speak to Him in prayer. For example, is it consistent to pray to God as "Lord" and then give Him a list of things we want Him to do for us? At such times, it would probably be more appropriate to address God as "Father" or "great Giver of life." If we are dealing with a spiritual warfare issue, a title such as "Lord of hosts" or "Mighty One" would be appropriate. When in pain or grief, we might address the Lord as "God of all comfort" or "God of hope" or "blessed Friend" or "the one who has promised never to leave us." Taking our cue from the Israelites and their sensitivity to the many characteristics of their beloved God, we should never speak His names or titles lightly.

Nehemiah's main request to God was that He remember His instructions to Moses: "If you are unfaithful, I will scatter you among the nations, but if you return to me and obey my commands, then even if your exiled people are at the farthest horizon, I will gather them from there and bring them to the place I have chosen as a dwelling for my Name" (Neh. 1:9). You can tell what is most on a person's heart by listening to what he or she prays. For Nehemiah, it was clearly the return of God's people.

Nehemiah prays 11 times in the short book of the Bible named for him. Not once does he mention the wall. The wall, it seems, was merely the project God gave Nehemiah to help bring the people back together. Nehemiah didn't pray about the project. He prayed about the longing of his heart. This is a remarkable distinctive of prayers in the New Testament as well: Pray-ers in the Bible never simply prayed for the project or event at hand. Their prayers always went beyond that, straight to the heart of the issue — straight from their heart to the heart of God.

PERSONAL APPROACH

Using Nehemiah's prayer as an example, compose a prayer to God regarding a situation that disturbs you:

Chapter Two

Learning from Paul

The Preventive Approach

What prompts you to pray for someone? Are you more apt to pray when someone is facing a crisis or an immediate need? Typically, our prayers are shortsighted in nature and focus on the physical rather than the spiritual. The Apostle Paul was prompted to go to prayer for unusual reasons and with kingdom results. How can we learn to pray beyond the immediate "answerables" to see long-range outcomes?

Read Ephesians 1:15-23.
Imagine that someone you greatly respect wrote this to you. How would you respond?

How or why are you usually prompted to pray for someone?

What prompted Paul to pray for the Ephesian believers?

Paul asked God to do something for the Ephesians *so that* something else would occur in their lives. What did Paul want to see happen? "I keep asking that the God of our Lord Jesus Christ, the glorious Father, may_____*so* *that*_____."

What would be the benefits in the lives of the Ephesians if that prayer was answered?

Would that prayer produce the same results if prayed for someone today?

Paul frequently prayed for one thing so that something else would occur. List the request and the desired result in the following passages:

Ephesians 3:16-19
Prayer

So that

Philippians 1:9-11
Prayer

So that

Colossians 1:9-14
Prayer

So that

Why do you think Paul did not pray for immediate physical needs, but for something with long-range results?

How will Paul's example shape your prayers for friends and loved ones?

A Closer Look

Read this statement and see if it sounds astonishing to you. "For this reason, ever since I heard about your faith in the Lord Jesus and your love for all the saints, I have not stopped giving thanks for you, remembering you in my prayers" (Eph. 1:15-16). Did you notice the connection between what Paul heard and the action he took? He heard about the faith and love of the Ephesian believers. Obviously, such news should cause one to give thanks, but why did this news cause Paul to pray for them?

Paul's prayer antennas picked up on the positive—"since I heard about your faith in the Lord Jesus and your love for all the saints." Most Christians today seem to view prayer as a problem-solver, therefore they wait until they hear of difficulties or a crisis before praying for a person or a group. However, Paul did not see problem solving as the primary purpose of prayer.

Instead, Paul, like Jesus, primarily used prayer as a problem-preventer rather than a problem-solver. A good example of this in Jesus' life was His prayer for His followers in John 17. The disciples had a lot of problems at that moment. For example, they were caught up with who among them was most important to Jesus. They were so self-centered that before the evening was over every one of them withdrew from Christ when He needed them most. Yet, Jesus did not mention any of these problems in His prayer. Instead, He prayed about the long-range issues that would make the disciples a powerful witness in the years to come—their protection, sanctification and unity.

Look at the catalyst for Paul's prayer for the people of Colossae. "You learned [the gospel] from Epaphras, our dear fellow servant, who is a faithful minister of Christ on our behalf, and who also told us of your love in the Spirit. For this reason, since the day we heard about you, we have not stopped praying for you." (Col. 1:7-9). What had Paul heard about these people? Their "love in the Spirit." That information was enough to launch Paul into interceding for the Colossians.

For the people of Ephesus, who were already known as people of faith and love, Paul asked God to give them "the Spirit of wisdom and revelation, so that" they would know God better. Also, that their spiritual eyes would be enlightened to know the hope, inheritance and power given to them. As you can see, none of these requests dealt with problems they were facing at that time.

Each of us has enough problems to keep counselors and intercessors busy for a lifetime. When we direct our prayers primarily toward problem solving, we enter a hopeless and endless tunnel. Christ did not come just to solve problems. He came to radically change lives into His image. That is why the New Testament prayers are primarily focused on the qualities that Jesus has.

In Charles Hummel's book *Tyranny of the Urgent*, he wrote how most people do not prioritize their lives to live by the important things. Therefore, the urgent things dictate how they live. He tells how Jesus gave His time and energy to that which had long-range importance. Jesus prayed the same way He lived—focused on the things that were eternally strategic. We can spend our time and energy praying for the endless problems people bring to us, or we can choose to pray about the strategic, long-range issues that can help form people into the image of Christ.

Why do we always ask each other, "What can I pray for you?" Ninety percent of the time people will tell us of a problem they are facing. Why? Probably because they want us to use prayer to solve their problems. Try something different. Instead of asking what others want you to pray, think of the long-range qualities that Jesus Christ has. Then ask God which of these qualities He wants to build into the life of your friend at this time. After God reveals which Christ-like qualities He desires for them, pray those things. Then the next time you see your friend, do what Paul did, tell them what you are praying. TAP God's resources for your friends.

T – *Think* of Christ's qualities.
A – *Ask* God which qualities He desires for your friend at this time.
P – *Pray* those qualities into your friend's life.

PERSONAL APPROACH
Who do you know that exemplifies faith and love? Compose a prayer to God for that person or group, using Paul's prayers as a guide.

Chapter Three

Learning from Jeremiah

The Heart-tuned Approach

Does God confuse you at times? Is it sometimes difficult to see how God is working in a situation? Every day as we read the newspaper or turn on the TV, we are confronted with what seems to be an endless parade of pointless tragedies. How do you pray when nothing makes sense?

Read Jeremiah 32.
What was happening to the country of Judah at the time Jeremiah prayed in verses 17-25?

In the midst of this national tragedy, Jeremiah was facing personal difficulties. How would you have responded in a similar situation?

What impresses you about Jeremiah's prayer in verses 17-25?

Did Jeremiah ask God to do anything specific?

Why do you think Jeremiah prayed this way?

Is prayer more than asking? What do you consider to be essential components of prayer?

How did God respond to Jeremiah's prayer? Does that surprise you?

A Closer Look
In the publisher's foreword to *If You Will Ask*, Oswald Chamber's thoughts are summarized as follows. "Prayer is getting ourselves attuned to God, not getting God attuned to us." This is a good statement to remember as we read Jeremiah's prayer (32:17-25) and consider his circumstances.

At the time of his prayer, Jeremiah was confined by King Zedekiah in the royal palace in Judah for conveying unpopular, but true, prophecies from God. A brutal enemy was about to climb over the wall, destroy the city, and capture what was left of God's chosen people. In the midst of all this, God sent a messenger to ask Jeremiah to buy a plot of ground in Judah—a land that He had said was about to be occupied by the Babylonian enemy!

How should we pray when nothing makes sense? What do we say when God acts in ways that seem out of character? Note what Jeremiah said to God in precisely this situation:

Ah, Sovereign LORD, *you have made the heavens and the earth by your great power and outstretched arm. Nothing is too hard for you. You show love to thousands but bring the punishment for the fathers' sins into the laps of their children after them. O great and powerful God, whose name is the* LORD *Almighty, great are your purposes and mighty are your deeds. Your eyes are open to all the ways of men; you reward everyone according to his conduct and as his deeds deserve. You performed miraculous signs and wonders in Egypt and have continued them to this day, both in Israel and among all mankind, and have gained the renown that is still yours. You brought your people Israel out of Egypt with signs and wonders, by a might hand and an outstretched arm and with great terror. You gave them this land you had sworn to give their forefathers, a land flowing with milk and honey. They came in and took possession of it, but they did not obey you or follow your law; they did not do what you commanded them to do. So you brought all this disaster upon them.*

See how the siege ramps are built up to take the city. Because of the sword, famine and plague, the city will be handed over to the Babylonians who are attaching it. What you said has happened, as you now see. And though the city will be handed over to the Babylonians, you, O Sovereign LORD, *say to me, "Buy the field with silver and have the transaction witnessed."*

Amazingly, in spite of all the chaos and mixed messages that were going on around him, Jeremiah did not ask God to do anything! He simply talked to God about who He was, what He had done in history, and what He was doing at that moment. In other words, *Jeremiah tuned his heart to God by talking to Him.*

Through this process of talking to God, Jeremiah was able to come to a clearer understanding of Him. When he better understood God, he was able to accept what God was doing—even though it was devastating. As Jeremiah prayed, recounting God's deeds as the Deliverer of the people of Israel, God's nature as Redeemer was reaffirmed. When God asked Jeremiah to buy a piece of land according to the ancient laws of redemption (Lev. 25:23-28), He planted a sign in the midst of Israel's destruction. It was a sign that He would one day redeem His people and bring them back to freedom in their homeland.

I used to get frustrated with God when He would do things that seemed contrary to what I knew of Him. Then one day, I said, "Lord, I want to know You as You realty are, not as I have always wanted You to be." The walls I had put around God came down. As long as I confined God to my small knowledge of Him, He frustrated me by going outside the walls of my understanding. Now, even though I do not always understand God's actions, I have peace that they are right and consistent with His nature. I know that what seems to be meaningless circumstances now will someday become meaningful.

Are you faced with circumstances that are making you feel confused, frustrated, or angry with God? Try talking it out with the Lord, as Jeremiah did, by recalling His character and action as revealed in the Bible, in history, and in your own life. In the midst of your despair, look for the promise of His redemption

---

PERSONAL APPROACH

Think of a difficult, seemingly meaningless circumstance that you, a friend, your church or your nation is facing. Using Jeremiah's prayer as an example, compose a prayer to God. Try to pray without asking God to do something.

Chapter Four

Learning from the Early Disciples

The Kingdom Approach

Peter and John were in a predicament. On their way to prayer at the Temple, a crippled beggar had approached them. Finding themselves without money to give him, Peter healed the man in Jesus name. They were seized and thrown into jail by the priests. Interrogated and threatened, they were finally released with orders not to speak or teach again in Jesus' name. Gathering the believer's together they held a prayer meeting and prayed a surprising prayer.

Read Acts 3-4:31. Re-read 4:24-30 as though you are one of the participants in this prayer meeting and it is *your* prayer.
If you had been part of this prayer meeting and knew that your life along with the lives of the other people, was threatened, what would you pray?

Why?

The disciples addressed God as "Sovereign Lord" in their prayer. In what ways was God's sovereignty recognized and acknowledged in their prayer?

Praying Scripture is a powerful way to pray. In what way did the disciples use Scripture in their prayer?

How did their prayer reflect a profound understanding and acceptance of their situation?

We can learn a lot by what pray-ers in the Bible did *not* pray. What things could the disciples have prayed but did not?

In light of their circumstances, why do you think the disciples asked God for boldness and signs and wonders instead of protection?

Frequently we hear of missionaries in foreign lands being arrested and thrown in prison for spreading the gospel. What types of things have you typically prayed for them in the past? In what ways will the way you pray for them change based on Acts 4:24-30?

A Closer Look

They were a small group of believers but they were growing and spreading. Now they received a serious threat—imprisonment or death if they spoke or taught at all in the name of Jesus. What does one do at a time of crisis? Look again at Acts 4:24-30. Imagine we are listening in on a group of first-century Christians praying in response to a life-threatening situation:

> *Sovereign Lord, . . . you made the heaven and the earth and the sea, and everything in them. You spoke by the Holy Spirit through the mouth of your servant, our father David: "Why do the nations rage and the peoples plot in vain? The kings of the earth take their stand and the rulers gather together against the Lord and against His Anointed One." Indeed Herod and Pontius Pilate met together with the Gentiles and the people of Israel in this city to conspire against your holy servant Jesus, whom you anointed. They did what your power and will have decided beforehand should happen. Now, Lord, consider their threats and enable your servants to speak your word with great boldness. Stretch out your hand to heal and perform miraculous signs and wonders through the name of your holy servant Jesus.*

Wait a minute! Did we hear right—their lives were threatened and they did not ask for protection? Wouldn't a more appropriate prayer have been, "O God, save us from these evil people. Don't let any harm come to us"?

Did you notice that they did not pray against those who threatened them. In fact, they did not pray against anything. They didn't even ask God to bind the strong man who obviously originated the idea of silencing them.

So far we have only observed what our friends in Acts did not pray—which of course is important when being mentored by such warriors of prayer. Let's focus our attention on how their prayer unfolds and what they *did* ask of God during this crisis.

We have to be impressed with their knowledge of Scripture and the way they used it in their prayer. Starting with the words of King David, they traced the sovereign work of God right up to events that took place only a couple months before they were threatened. They saw once again that no one can thwart God's plan and purpose.

It was obvious to them that even the unjust way Herod and Pilate treated Jesus was "decided beforehand" by the Lord. If in God's plan His Son did not avoid suffering, perhaps they should not ask for better treatment. With this perspective they could see that those who threatened them were but tools in the Sovereign Lord's hand.

With this encouragement, this group of believers simply asked themselves, "What do we need in order to best co-labor with God in His sovereign work on earth?" The answer to that question became their prayer request, "enable your servants to speak your word with great boldness. Stretch out your hand to heal and perform miraculous signs and wonders through the name of your holy servant Jesus."

When you or I face a crisis, how are we going to pray? God may not lead us to ask the same specific requests these early disciples asked. However, we do need to learn from them how to see our situation from God's perspective. Asking is the easy part of praying. Knowing what to ask takes time and reasoning with God through the Scriptures. A good starting place would be to ask God the question, "Amid this crisis, what do I need in order to best co-labor with You, Lord, in Your sovereign work on earth?" Seek to join God in His purposes. Look to Him as opposed to looking for the easy way out!

PERSONAL APPROACH

Think of a crisis situation in the life of a believer. Using the disciple's prayer as an example, draft a prayer of your own:

Chapter Five

Learning from David

The Thoughtful Approach

Meditative prayer. Have you ever tried it? Have you ever taken time to think long and deep about God, about His name or one of His many titles? Have you contemplated the magnitude of God's universe until spontaneous praise erupts from your soul? Praise is not just emotion, it is an intelligent response to who God is.

Read Psalm 8 thoughtfully.
If this was the only passage of Scripture you had ever read, what could you know about God?

What can you know about human beings from this psalm?

David wrote: "When I consider your heavens . . ." (v. 3). Using an encyclopedia, a science book, or the internet, gather some facts about the vastness of the universe. Use those facts to prompt praise as you meditate.

> Example: our galaxy (Milky Way) is 100,000 light years wide. A single light year is equal to six trillion miles. The galaxy nearest to us, Andromeda, is 2.5 million light years away. Telescopes can pick up approximately 100,000,000,000 galaxies but beyond that we do not know how many galaxies make up the universe. Yet God measures universe in the span of His hand! (Is. 40:12).

What does His creation say about Him?

Tell Him how the universe makes you feel.

A Closer Look

Mike's letter came as a pleasant surprise. We are good friends and we had often expressed our appreciation for each other. But when he wrote a long letter telling me in specific detail what I had meant to him these past 10 years, I was touched and honored.

It wasn't a special occasion. It wasn't my birthday or a celebration of a significant achievement. Mike had just been thinking about me and felt the need to express his thoughts. That, in my mind, made what he said all the more special.

Thoughtful, unsolicited praise. That's what David wrote to God in Psalm 8. It was like a friend writing, "You were so much on my mind, I just had to write and tell you."

Psalm 8 was not an emotional outburst. David was thinker. If he awoke in the night, he would meditate (see Ps. 63:6). He often told

God how he meditated, thought on, and remembered Him. Psalm 8 came out of such a time. It was as though David had lingered so long on the name, *Yahweh*, that his thoughts required verbal expression. The words just flowed out of him: "O LORD, our Lord, how majestic is your name in all the earth!"

God's name is *Yahweh* (translated LORD in the English translations of the Bible). This name is derived from who He is. Most of His other titles come from what He does. *Yahweh* means I AM. The self-existent One. He who was and is and will be. The only uncreated being, complete within Himself, needing nothing outside Himself to be more sufficient or whole. No other being could ever call himself simply "I AM."

The longer David meditated on God's name, the more praise welled up within him. Notice that David began and ended his written praise by acknowledging the awesomeness of God's name. Everything else in the psalm has significance because of who God is. If God's name were not majestic, then mentioning children praising and humans ruling would be a hollow exercise. But sandwiched between these exaltations of God's name, they become words of praise.

"From the lips of children and infants you have ordained praise because of your enemies, to silence the foe and the avenger" (v. 2). David was astonished that the All-sufficient God would entrust His work to children and infants. Children are created beings. Infants are helpless. Children have to be warned and protected against a wide variety of dangers. David praised God because He needed no help whatsoever to accomplish His purposes, yet He ordained the most helpless on earth to silence His enemies.

David's meditative praise continued as he contemplated the universe created by God's fingers. Nothing brings God's vastness into perspective like considering the universe. I will never forget a time of praise with a group in Africa. We were dwelling on God's greatness when a professor began describing back to God how massive His universe was. We paused to let the professor give us more information. With added understanding, we were able to worship with a sense of astonishment—not the universe, but the God who created it.

David's meditation on the universe caused him to exclaim, "What is man that you are mindful of him, the son of man that you care for him?" (v. 4). Look, as David obviously did, at the contrasts.

The All-sufficient God uses helpless infants. And though the universe is the largest of God's creation, it is human beings that He is "mindful of." Why? Because He made us in His image, only "a little lower than God" (v. 5, NASB). Of all His creation, God crowned humans "with glory and majesty."

David was overwhelmed by the thought that human beings are God's favorite creation. He was inspired by God's evidence of trust in humans: "You made him ruler over the works of your hands; you put everything under his feet" (v. 6). David gave high praise to God because his heart and mind had given serious thought to the One who could do it all Himself, yet nevertheless assigned the task.

Psalm 8 is a great model of a prayer of meditative praise. I want to encourage you to learn how to praise God through meditation. Don't just do a study. Meditate. Think prayerfully. Linger on one of God's titles long enough that you become astonished at who He is. Once you have some understanding of what a particular title says about who God is, start thinking about what happens *as a result of* who He is.

It doesn't have to be a special occasion. Warm God's heart with thoughtful, unsolicited praise.

PERSONAL APPROACH
Read Psalm 8 to God as from your heart. Compose your own psalm to God.

Chapter Six

Learning from a Tax Collector

The Humble Approach

Throughout Scripture, it is clear that God puts a premium on humility. Listed as one of the three good things that God requires of us (Mic. 6:8), humility is exemplified in Jesus Christ Himself (Phil. 2:8). In James 4:6 we find a clear distinction in how God views pride and humility. God opposes the proud. The Greek word for *opposes* is *antitasso* which is a military term meaning "to set oneself in battle formation against." "God sets himself in battle formation against the proud . . . so humble yourselves before God." In contrast, God saves, guides, sustains and gives grace to the humble (Ps. 18:27, 25:9, 147:6; Prov. 3:34).

And here is the spiritual paradox: the very act of bringing yourself low will cause you to be lifted up (Lk. 14:11).

Read Luke 18:9-14.
What assumptions did the Pharisee make about:
Himself?

Others?

God?

What assumptions did the tax collector make about:
Himself?

God?

Although the tax collector did not make mention of others in his prayer, how do you think he viewed others as he prayed?

What basic beliefs do you think contributed to the assumptions of these two men?

Why do you think that the tax collector specifically asked for mercy?

Why not something like forgiveness or blessing?

Read 2 Corinthians 5:21 and Hebrews 10:19.
What has Jesus accomplished for us? How should these verses affect our prayers?

Can you think of any example(s) in your prayer life where you have fallen into the category of the Pharisee or tax collector?

A Closer Look

From time to time, God seems distant to me. During one such time, I became desperate. I got up in middle of the night and went over to our church building. I explained to God that I desperately needed Him to tell me what was wrong. What did I need to do to draw close to Him again? For an hour or so I was silent, waiting for God's Spirit to reveal the sin or any other barrier that was producing distance between us. Nothing. God was as silent as I was.

Finally, I said, "Lord, let me tell You what I think the problem might be." I confessed something about myself that I thought probably offended God. This confession reminded me of something else, which reminded me of something else, which in turn reminded me of something else. Suddenly, my mind seemed aware of every sin and problem in my life. I felt myself spiraling downward until I felt filthy and dirty before the Holy One.

At this low point, I cried out, "O God, I'm a sinner through and through." For the first time that night, God spoke to me. He helped me see two things about myself. First, He affirmed that I was indeed a sinner through and through. Second, He pointed out how self-righteous I was.

My thinking always had been that I had to do something to earn a closeness to God. Perhaps, for instance, if I confessed enough sins, or at least the right ones, God would welcome me into His most holy place. That night, God revealed to me that the only way to Him is through the blood of Christ (Heb. 10:19). The very best I have to offer the Lord, no matter how good it may look to others, is like filthy rags without the saving blood of Christ (Is. 64:6).

Jesus told a story to a group of self-righteous people: "Two men went up to the temple to pray, one a Pharisee and the other a tax collector. The Pharisee stood up and prayed about himself: 'God, I thank you that I am not like other men—robbers, evildoers, adulterers—or even like this tax collector. I fast twice a week and give a tenth of all I get.' But the tax collector stood at a distance. He would not even look up to heaven, but beat his breast and said, 'God, have mercy on me, a sinner'" (Lk. 18:10-13).

The tax collector's prayer is one of the shortest yet most meaningful prayers in the Bible. Jesus strongly favored it. Why? Because the tax collector humbly admitted the truth about himself. He was a sinner. He did not confess his individual sins, but that he was a sinner. He could stop doing certain sins on his own, but he could not change the fact that he was a sinner. This truth led him to ask for the one thing that could help him: God's mercy.

A friend of mine, who is sensitive to the strengths and weaknesses of the church in America, said that the greatest problem in the church today is our self-righteousness. I agree. We seem to be engaged in an endless endeavor to do enough of the right things so God will have to bless us. If we get enough people to pray across America, then God will have to send revival. If we just get the right programs in place, God will make our church grow.

We, like the Pharisee, try to justify ourselves before God. Although we may not use the exact words, some of our prayers come close to saying: "God, I thank you that I am not like 'so and so' (here we usually insert the name of someone we consider to be in blatant sin)"—while God waits to hear our plea for mercy.

Oswald Chambers wrote: "If the Spirit of God has given you a vision of what you are apart from the grace of God, you know there is no criminal who is half so bad in actuality as you know yourself to be in possibility" (*My Utmost for His Highest*, June 1). That night, alone in our church building, I understood the truth of Chambers' statement. In brokenness, I admitted that I am a sinner. For the first time in my life, I realized that if any good comes to me, it comes as an act of mercy on God's part.

Jesus' conclusion to the story He told is this: "For everyone who exalts himself will be humbled, and he who humbles himself will be exalted" (Lk. 18:14). If we want God's favor and blessing, the starting place is to humbly admit our desperate need for His mercy. Then we can accept what God accepts: the finished work of Christ.

Has self-righteousness crept into your life? Are you able to pray, "God, have mercy on me, a sinner"? If not, humble yourself before God, pray that sinner's prayer, and experience the power of His blood and mercy.

PERSONAL APPROACH

Think about what you life might look like apart from God's mercy. Write a letter of thanks to our merciful God.

Chapter Seven

Learning from Solomon

The Wise Approach

Literally a dream come true. The Lord appears to you in a dream and says, "Ask Me for anything you want. . . ." What will it be? Wealth? Long life? How about revenge on your enemies?

As tempting as it might be for any of us to ask for these things, Solomon displayed wisdom in his request even before he asked for it. And even while he slept! "So give your servant a discerning heart to govern your people and to distinguish between right and wrong. For who is able to govern this great people of yours?" (1 K. 3:9; see vv. 3-15). He woke to find that not only had the Lord granted his request for wisdom—he received riches and honor as well.

Read 1 Kings 8:22-61.
In this account, Solomon is using his God-given wisdom as he prays. Go back through Solomon's prayer and mark things that show Solomon's foresight and wisdom in the things he asked.

What things had Solomon wisely observed about God that influenced his prayer?

What things had Solomon wisely observed about human nature that influenced his prayer?

If Solomon was your mentor and you were there with him during the dedication of the temple, what could you learn about him from the way he talked to God?

What could you learn about God from the way Solomon talked with Him?

What could you learn about talking to God from his prayer?

Make a summarized list of the specific requests that Solomon asked of God.

A Closer Look

I have a friend who is a very gifted communicator. Even when people strongly disagree with his worldview, they are still drawn to interact with him. I'm impressed with his wisdom.

I love to pray with this friend. The first time we prayed together, it was evident that he was no novice at communicating with God. It was then that I learned that wisdom is as important in talking with God as it is in talking with people.

We don't have to read much of King Solomon's writings to understand why he has been called the wisest man who ever lived. All of us have good hindsight. Wisdom has good foresight.

Wisdom is the ability to properly apply knowledge and understanding. It can look at circumstances and make good choices. Solomon did this in his praying as well as his decision-making as a king.

In the New Testament, the Apostle Paul wrote about the importance of praying with the mind as well as the spirit: "I will pray with my spirit, but I will also pray with my mind" (1 Cor. 14:15). Solomon's example in 1 Kings 8 can help us learn to pray more fruitfully with the mind.

Solomon had finished building a temple for the God of Israel. After blessing all the leaders of Israel, he got on his knees, lifted his hands toward heaven, and prayed, "O LORD, God of Israel, there is no God like you in heaven above or on earth below—you who keep your covenant of love with your servants who continue wholeheartedly in your way" (1 K. 8:23). God has many titles and descriptions, but Solomon did not randomly choose one. He thoughtfully addressed God in a way that was consistent with what he wanted to ask of Him, calling Him the God who keeps His covenant of love with those who continue wholeheartedly in His way.

A summary of Solomon's requests is found in verse 30: "Hear the supplication of your servant and of your people Israel when they pray toward this place. Hear from heaven, your dwelling place, and when you hear, forgive." Wisely, Solomon built his entire prayer around his knowledge of God and people. He described seven potential scenarios in which the people would need to pray for help. He was acknowledging before God and the people that they would be dependent upon Him to hear and forgive.

Solomon had the foresight to know that God's people would stray from being obedient to His law. He also knew that, in keeping with His character of love, the Lord would pressure His people to turn back through various circumstances. Solomon understood that eventually God's people would cry out to Him. Therefore, 12 times Solomon asked God to "hear" His people. Six times he asked God to "forgive" the people when they turned to Him for help.

When Jesus was on earth, He asked a lot of questions. It was His way of stimulating thought in people, a way of encouraging wisdom. God created us as beings who can reason. It is an honor to Him when we take the time and effort to think about what we are going to say to Him. Lazy, thoughtless prayer is a dishonor to God.

How can we be wise in our prayers? First of all, think about who God is in connection with the need that is before you. As Nehemiah taught us in chapter one, to properly address God takes thought. Don't get stuck on just one way of addressing God. Do Him the honor of thinking more fully about who He is before you pray.

James Fraser was a missionary who saw thousands of Chinese come to Christ. He wrote: "I also find it helpful to make a short list, like notes prepared for a sermon, before every season of prayer. The mind needs to be guided as well as the spirit attuned. I can thus get my thoughts in order, and having prepared my prayer can put the notes on the table or chair before me, kneel down and get to business" (*The Prayer of Faith*, p. 14).

Think also about the people for whom you have a responsibility. Where are they vulnerable? What can you pray that will help them if or when they fall? What aspect of the kingdom do they need? What will they need God to do for them? Sometimes it has helped me to write out my prayers for these people.

May God give you the courage and willingness to expend effort in praying wisely and thoughtfully.

PERSONAL APPROACH

Use your summarized list of Solomon's requests as a prayer guide to pray for a group of Christians—perhaps those at your church. Think through each prayer point. Personalize the wisdom in your prayer for your specific group.

Chapter Eight

Learning from Epaphras

The Zealous Approach

Little is mentioned about Epaphras in Scripture. From the few words penned by Paul in Colossians and Philemon, we find that he was faithful, a teacher, a servant, always thinking of others, self-sacrificing, and a zealous prayer warrior (Col. 1:7, 4:12; Phlm. 1:23).

He came from Colossae, and he prayed for his own people—his friends, relatives, and brothers/sisters in Christ. We don't have a record of prayers he might have made for foreign mission fields. But we do know he became a prayer warrior for the people in his sphere of influence.

Write a list of people in your sphere of influence: friends, relatives, brothers/sisters in Christ, etc. Keep this list in front of you as you learn from Epaphras' prayer.

Read Colossians 4:12.

When you think of someone "wrestling in prayer," what do you visualize?

What circumstances would require someone to wrestle in prayer?

Epaphras prayed that his friends would "stand firm in all the will of God." What would the answer to that prayer look like?

What qualities did Epaphras possess that made him an excellent prayer warrior (Col. 1:7, 4:12; Phlm. 1:23)?

What qualities do you possess that will make you an excellent prayer warrior?

A Closer Look

A dear intercessor calls my wife and me regularly to tell what she is praying for us. Recently, she shared a certain passage of Scripture, which she had been praying for me regularly regarding an important need. I was encouraged to know exactly what she was praying for and that she was praying so fervently for me. It gave me a sense of hope and expectation that God was going to work in that area of my life.

The Christians in the city of Colossae must have had this same experience, for they had received word from the Apostle Paul that their friend Epaphras was praying for them. Moreover, Paul told them exactly what Epaphras was asking God to do: "Epaphras, who is one of your number, a bondslave of Jesus Christ, sends you his greetings, always laboring earnestly for you in his prayers, that you may stand perfect and fully assured in all the will of God" (Col. 4:12, NASB).

It is easy to imagine that Paul often prayed with Epaphras. Paul noticed two things about his friend's prayers. Whenever they got around to praying for the Christians in Colossae, Epaphras began praying with more energy. Paul also noticed that Epaphras had a specific prayer for his friends in his home city: that they would "stand perfect and fully assured in all the will of God."

Epaphras' prayers for his friends were not casual. They were energetic, fervent, and costly. His manner of praying was described as "laboring earnestly." Some translations say he was "wrestling in prayer." This is an athletic term. It is the effort of a runner who is trying to win first place. It is the determination of a wrestler refusing to be pinned. Paul used this same expression in 1 Corinthians 9:25 when he described an athlete who "competes" to win a prize.

Epaphras was not the first person to ask something of God that required labor in prayer. Moses spent 40 days fasting and praying for God to forgive Israel (Exodus 32). When Daniel prayed for God to have mercy on Israel, he "turned to the Lord God and pleaded with him in prayer and petition, in fasting, and in sackcloth and ashes" (Dan. 9:3). Even the Lord Jesus "offered up prayers and petitions with loud cries and tears" (Heb. 5:7).

It seems that some answers to prayer cannot be obtained by casually asking. There are some requests that, when answered, will radically change people's lives. Such prayers are significant enough to meet opposition and therefore are costly to the pray-er.

What Epaphras asked God to do, in fact, required nothing less than changing the will of human beings. Think about that. When Jesus spoke to the wind and waves, they obeyed Him immediately. Human cells changed instantly when He spoke to the sick, blind, and deaf. The devil and his demons had no choice but to obey our Lord's commands. But when the Lord of heaven and earth spoke to human beings, it was possible for them to say "no." I believe that the greatest resistance to God's kingdom on earth is not the powers of darkness, but the human will.

Epaphras prayed that the Colossians would "stand perfect and fully assured in all the will of God." Bending human will to God's will is a costly process. No one understood this better than Jesus in Gethsemane. In order for the Son of God to stand completely in His Father's will, He spent three agonizing hours in prayer. No one can be perfect and fully assured in all the will of God without losing his or her own will. That takes labor-intensive prayer.

When the Apostle Paul wrote to the church in Colossae, he was able to tell them exactly what Epaphras "always" prayed for them. A good parallel is the story of Zechariah (Luke 1). An angel came to him and said, "Do not be afraid, Zechariah; your prayer has been heard" (v. 13). If an angel came and told you that the Lord had heard your prayer, wouldn't you wonder which prayer he was talking about? There was no question in Zechariah's mind, for one prayer had burned deeply in his and Elizabeth's hearts for years—a prayer for a child.

Epaphras had that same kind of burning prayer for the Colossians. He always asked that they would "stand perfect and fully assured in all the will of God."

Have you become too casual in your praying? What are you asking God to do that requires you to labor earnestly in prayer? Can you identify your specific prayer for the various people in your life?

PERSONAL APPROACH

List some things that you know are God's will. Take your list and try using it to "wrestle in prayer" for the people who mean a lot to you.

Chapter Nine

Learning from Hannah

The Grieving Approach

Is there any more excruciating emotion than grief? It is raw and human—an emotion with which our Lord clearly identified (Lk 19:41; Jn 11:35).

Several years ago, I spoke to a group of 40 middle-aged people. I asked how many of them had a desire of which they had been praying for many years and still had no answer. All 40 of them raised their hands. I raised my hand as well. For 20 years I have pleaded with God for one of the deepest longings of my heart. There have been times when I've hurt so deeply I could not form words.

Read 1 Samuel 1:1-20.
What do you think drove Hannah to keep praying? Why didn't she give up?

What do you think Hannah believed about God? How did that influence her prayers?

Why do you think God withheld a child from Hannah for so many years?

How did surrender figure into Hannah's prayer and God's answer?

What do you long to see God do?

Are you willing to keep on praying and not give up?

What do you need to help you persevere?

Knowing what you know about God, can you see that there might be a reason for God's delay in bringing an answer to your request?

In your situation, what might surrender look like?

A Closer Look

The story of Hannah in 1 Samuel 1 gives us a vivid picture of answered prayer that comes out of a long period of grief. God had done two things in Hannah's life: He gave her a desire to be a mother, and, at the same time, He "closed her womb." Because of this conflict, Hannah lived in grief and frustration. Her husband's other wife had several sons and daughters, and she mocked Hannah for her infertility. At every turn, Hannah was reminded of her shame over not being able to bear children. Though her husband, Elkanah, deeply loved her, her grief seemed unbearable.

Every year Elkanah took his family to Shiloh to worship and make sacrifices. Hannah would go to the house of the Lord there to weep and pray for a child. I've often wondered how many different ways she thought of to ask God for a child. How many sins did she think of to confess, hoping that something would bring an answer from God? But no matter how she prayed, God was silent. We are told that this went on "year after year."

Another year passed, and they all went again to Shiloh. Hannah went to the house of the Lord to pour out her heart: "In bitterness of soul Hannah wept much and prayed to the LORD" (1 Sam. 1:10). The many years of sorrow and grief had driven Hannah to such despair that she then made an unbelievable vow to God. Her prayer is recorded for us: "O LORD Almighty, if you will only look upon your servant's misery and remember me, and not forget your servant but give her a son, then I will give him to the LORD for all the days of his life, and no razor will ever be used on his head" (v. 11).

It was this prayer that God answered. Hannah conceived and Samuel was born. After weaning him, she gave the boy to God to serve in the house of the Lord, and Samuel become the prophet-ruler of Israel from his youth to his old age.

Consider the remarkable long-range impact of Hannah's prayer. Because Hannah gave Samuel over to God, an entire generation of Israelites was saved under his leadership. But it was despair that drove Hannah to pray that prayer of total surrender. Had God answered Hannah's first or second appeal for a child, she may not have given him over to God. Samuel would not have become the prophet-ruler he became, and a generation of Israelites might have lived under the oppressive rule of one of their enemies (see 1 Sam. 12:11).

There are two lessons we can learn from Hannah's experience and her prayer. First, our Sovereign Lord has long-range, beautiful plans. We, like Hannah, see only the immediate things around us. Oftentimes, God has to bring pain or grief into our lives to bring us to the place where we can pray as Hannah did—a prayer of surrender that gives back to God what He gives to us.

Second, to really know God, we need to observe Him over a long period of time. It's an injustice to Him to take a snapshot at any given moment. Hannah's initial experience with God made God seem cruel or withholding. But by the time you get to the end of Samuel's life, you see God's incredible foresight and mercy for an entire nation.

Hannah's psalm of praise in 1 Samuel 2 shows us what she learned about God through her long and painful experience. She proclaims, "There is no one holy like the LORD" (v. 2). "The LORD sends poverty and wealth; he humbles and he exalts. He raises the poor from the dust and lifts the needy from the ash heap" (vv. 7-8).

Are you experiencing distress, grief, or confusion that you know God could resolve quickly, but at this moment He is neither speaking nor acting on your behalf? I plead with you to hold on to the truth that God is merciful—and has a long-range purpose for your every prayer longing.

PERSONAL APPROACH
Fashion your own prayer using Hannah's as a model (1 Sam. 1:11).

Chapter Ten

Learning from Isaac

The Blessing Approach

The sibling rivalry in your family has gotten out of hand. Your favorite son was duped out of his inheritance by your wife's favorite son. Not only did the usurper cheat and lie to get his way, he took advantage of your age and handicaps in the process. He even enlisted your own wife to help in the plan to deceit. Now the deceived son is threatening to murder the deceiver and the deceiver is planning to flee the country. Before he leaves, however, you feel compelled to pray for him.

This was exactly the situation in which Isaac found himself. Competitive since the womb, his twin sons Esau and Jacob were going at it tooth and nail. The situation was desperate and called for desperate prayer.

If you were in his shoes, what would you pray?

Read Genesis 25:19-28:3,4.

What was Isaac's son, Jacob, like?

How did Isaac feel about Jacob and what he had done to Esau?

As Isaac prayed for Jacob, he did not focus on his immediate needs or his character flaws. What was the focus of Isaac's prayer for Jacob? What would the answer to his prayer look like?

Look up Genesis 17:1 where God first called Himself El Shaddai. What were the circumstances there?

Why do you think Isaac addressed God as El Shaddai, "God Almighty," as he prayed for Jacob?

Think of someone you have prayed for whose life seems hopeless. What things have you been praying for that person? How are those things similar/dissimilar to the things Isaac prayed for Jacob?

A Closer Look

What would you pray if your child were in danger and leaving home and you did not know if you would ever see him or her again? Would you pray for God's immediate protection or His blessings for future fruitfulness? Isaac focused on the future. Although his prayer was short, it is one of the most far-reaching prayers in the Bible. It is still being answered today.

May God Almighty bless you. In Hebrew, God Almighty (El Shaddai) means, among other things, the All Sufficient One. It indicates that He is the fulfillment of all needs. The first time God introduced Himself as El Shaddai was when Sarah could no longer bear children (Gen. 17:1). Sarah and Abraham had reached the end of their human resources in this department. Then God appeared as the All Sufficient One who could and would give them a child. Isaac was that child. No doubt he had heard his parents tell the story of El Shaddai over and over. Now Isaac was asking that his son, Jacob, would have a firsthand experience with El Shaddai.

Isaac's prayer continued: "And make you fruitful and increase your numbers until you become a community of peoples." It would have covered the bases to simply pray that God would bless Jacob. But something compelled Isaac to pray for more. He prayed that his son would be fruitful. He asked for grandchildren and great-grandchildren. His ultimate request was that Jacob would become a community of peoples!

Where did Isaac come up with such an audacious prayer? It seems he understood an important truth about the Lord.

After God created Adam and Eve, His first action was to bless them by saying, "Be fruitful and increase in number; fill the earth" (Gen. 1:28). He gave the same blessing to Noah, Abraham, Isaac, and Jacob. It is a blessing of generations. God made this very clear when He changed Abram's name (exalted father) to Abraham (father of a multitude). Although Genesis is a book about beginnings, the terms "descendants" and "generations" appear 75 times. The Creator God is a generational God! Isaac understood that God's blessing on mankind meant more than an individual's fruitfulness or health.

Twenty years after Isaac's prayer of blessing, Jacob started the long journey back home. He would be returning home with a large family and hundreds of livestock. Surely he was blessed with many things. Yet when Jacob met God along the road, he wrestled with Him all night saying, "I will not let you go unless you bless me" (Gen. 32:26). He understood that the real blessing of God went beyond personal fruitfulness. He would only be fully blessed when God made him into a multitude of people.

A while back, a friend and I were talking about how the God of the Bible is a generational God. After an enlightening conversation, we began to pray. We both have dear friends who have wandered from God. As usual, we asked the Lord to draw them back to Himself as we claimed the victories of Christ over the enemy of their souls. As we prayed, God reminded us of His desire for the generations. We quickly realized that we had been so caught up with our friends' immediate needs that we had never asked the Lord to do anything beyond them. So we began to ask with confidence that our generational God would bless our friends in such a way that they would be fruitful and multiply and become a multitude of people.

Will you ask *beyond* the needs of those for whom you pray? We all have "Jacobs" in our lives whose immediate concerns threaten to commandeer our attention. Let us follow Isaac's faithful example, however. Let us remember to pray that God will raise up future generations through those whose lives seem hopeless right now.

PERSONAL APPROACH
Use Isaac's prayer of Genesis 28:3 as a guide to help you pray expectantly for someone in a desperate situation. When God answers your prayer, what do you think His answer will look like?

Chapter Eleven

Learning from Jesus
The Long-Range Approach

The path of least resistance. Isn't that really what we hope for, pray for? When hardships or suffering threaten our family, our friends, or us isn't it natural to want to "pray it all away"?

Jesus clearly taught us to pray, "deliver us from the evil one" (Mt. 6:13b). He also prayed in earnest for us that God the Father would "protect [us] from the evil one" (Jn. 17:15). As we follow His instructions and use His model of intercession, these examples will undoubtedly shape our prayers.

But there was a time when Jesus prayed differently. There was a time when He did not try to neutralize the effects of the enemy as he attacked a dear friend.

Read Luke 22:14-34.
Describe what was happening when Jesus prayed for Simon Peter.

Read Job 1 and 2.
Compare/contrast what happened to Peter and Job. How are the situations different? How are they similar?

Do you think situations like these still occur today?

If you had been there and knew that Satan wanted to sift your friend, how would you have prayed?

Peter was in training as a future leader of the church. Read what Peter wrote in 1 Peter 1:6-7. What do you think he learned from the way Jesus prayed for him and from the experience of his denial?

Read 1 Peter 5:8-9.
What benefits do you think Peter experienced as a result of the way Jesus prayed?

Read 1 Corinthians 5:5.

What other ways might God allow the enemy to be used in someone's life?

If Jesus had never prayed the way He did, what might have been different in Peter's life? How might that have affected us today?

Do you find this type of praying to be difficult? Why or why not?

A Closer Look

It was the last evening before the Lord Jesus Christ was to die the cruel death of crucifixion. Within hours, Jesus would be arrested, falsely accused, and nailed to a cross. He was having a meal with His 12 closest friends, but it was not what you'd call a peaceful evening. Everything around Him was falling apart. Judas was about to betray Him. It looked as though three years of work would be lost. Jesus' soul, understandably, was "overwhelmed with sorrow to the point of death" (Mk. 14:34). As if that weren't enough, the disciples were arguing over which of them was the greatest.

It is at this moment that Jesus makes a remark that seems totally out of context. In the middle of responding to the question of who shall be greatest, Jesus tells His soon-to-be forsakers, "You are those who have stood by me in my trials" (Lk. 22:28). It was so like the Lord to see good in people—even when they were acting contrary to His needs.

Except for Jesus, every person in the room was consumed with himself. Jesus, however, was thinking about His friends. How would they survive what was about to take place? So He singled out the one person who was most sure of himself and said, "Simon, Simon, Satan has asked to sift you as wheat. But I have prayed for you, Simon, that your faith may not fail. And when you have turned back, strengthen your brothers" (vv. 31-32).

What do we usually do when one of our friends is under the attack of Satan? Most of us respond by taking a stand against the evil one. We work to remove the attack. We need to understand, however, that *God has a purpose for Satan*. The Lord can use our enemy to make us better people! Jesus understood the usefulness of Satan. He had seen it in the wilderness three years earlier. He knew that what the devil means for evil, God can use for good.

In some ways, Simon Peter faced a situation similar to Job's. Satan asked permission to tempt Simon, hoping to prove to God that he was more chaff than wheat. God took the challenge in order to turn Peter into a man of faith. This was a risk, for Peter was very self-confident. His first words of reply to Jesus, in fact, were, "Lord, I am ready to go with you to prison and to death" (v. 33). But God had a plan: He was going to use Satan to sift out Simon Peter's self-confidence and replace it with God-confidence.

Jesus went for the long-range solution to Peter's dilemma rather than focusing on the short-term problem. In doing so, he allowed Peter to do the unthinkable: to deny Christ. Amazing as it sounds, Jesus was less concerned about Peter denying Him than He was about what Peter would do after the denial! The moment of crisis came after the third denial, when the rooster crowed. Peter could have walked off, angry with himself and too proud and embarrassed to admit he had failed. Instead, Jesus' prayer was answered. The words of his Lord flooded Peter's mind, causing him to go outside and weep bitterly (v. 62).

The rest of the story is recorded in the book of Acts. Peter became what Jesus prayed for: a man of faith. Then, in one of his own letters, Peter wrote: "In this you greatly rejoice, though now for a little while you may have had to suffer grief in all kinds of trials. These have come so that your faith—of greater worth than gold, which perishes even though refined by fire—may be proved genuine and may result in praise, glory and honor when Jesus Christ is revealed" (1 Pet. 1:6-7).

Many Christians try to use prayer as a tool to rescue their friends from harm, pain, or grief. Jesus used prayer to build the quality of the eternal into Peter's life. As our Intercessor, the Lord Jesus continues to pray the same for us today. In some situations of attack, if we could hear His prayers for us, we might be disappointed. "Lord," we might cry, "You have the power to deliver me from the attacks of the enemy. Don't let him harass me." Jesus, however, keeps praying, "Father, don't let his faith fail, but use this attack to purify his faith."

I have often wondered what Peter would have been like if Jesus had resisted Satan instead of praying for Peter's faith. Do you know anyone who is currently under attack from the evil one? Before you quickly take a stand against Satan, stop and ask God if He is using this in any way for the benefit of the one being attacked. If you sense that He is, consider joining the Lord in praying that the faith of this saint will not fail and that he or she will be further purified for Jesus.

PERSONAL APPROACH

Think of someone who is under attack from Satan. Spend some time asking God about the best way to pray for him or her. Use Luke 22:31–32 or John 17:15 as you are led to shape a prayer for them.

Chapter Twelve

Learning from Moses
The Intercession Approach

What would motivate you to challenge God on behalf of a group of whining, grumbling people? Would you wash your hands of the whole complaining brood, or would you stand your ground in the face of the Lord's anger?

Moses found himself arguing with God over an ungrateful bunch of ex-slaves. In the middle of their deliverance and God's miraculous provision, they decided they had waited long enough for Moses' return from the mountain. Although they had repeatedly seen evidence that the God of Moses was the one true God, they quickly turned to a handmade replacement that would be there at their beck and call.

God had every right to be angry. He had every right to destroy them and make Moses into a mighty nation to fulfill His purposes. But Moses went to bat for them.

Read Exodus 32.
Describe in your own words what was happening in Israel's camp (vv. 1-6).

Moses' prayer of intercession recorded in Exodus 32:11-13 indicates that Moses believed some very specific things about God that caused him to pray this way. What were they?

How did Moses reason with God?

In verse 11 we are told that Moses sought the favor of the Lord as he interceded. Read Exodus 33:12-14. What part did Moses' relationship with God play in the way he approached Him in prayer?

We, the church, often stray from the Lord. What are some idols we have in our lives today?

A Closer Look

The passage from Exodus recounts how Moses rescued approximately three million of God's people by interceding for them. This great prayer took place on Mount Sinai when he received the Ten Commandments. The people of Israel had not heard from God or Moses for 40 days and had taken matters into their own hands. They created an idol that stole their hearts away from God. Moses pleaded with God—and God listened.

We can learn three important lessons about intercession from Moses' example. First, Moses received his information from God. If God had not spoken, Moses would not have known what Israel had done or the awfulness of their sin. God's insight alone drove Moses to prayer.

The human view of things is often shallow. We need to wait on God to discern what He thinks and feels about particular situations. We must learn to listen to God in Scripture and in silence.

Second, Moses was deeply concerned about God's reputation on earth. He could not tolerate the thought that the Egyptians might misjudge the faithfulness of God or His intentions for His people. Therefore, Moses reasoned with God on the basis of what God could lose if He did not take action.

Think of today's world. Because many of God's followers are unholy, people don't see the holiness of the Lord. Because we attempt to live self-sufficient lives, our God is not known as all sufficient. The Lord's name is polluted on earth. For the sake of our Lord's reputation, we must appeal to Him to reveal our sins and turn all hearts toward Himself.

One final lesson from Moses: His plea was based upon God's promise to Abraham. In essence, he held God to His word. God loves it when His children believe His promises enough to remind Him of them. Dawson Trotman, founder of The Navigators, said that the need of the hour was "an army of soldiers, dedicated to Jesus Christ, who believe not only that He is God, but that He can fulfill every promise He has ever made, and that there isn't anything too hard for Him" (from *The Need of the Hour*).

According to Ezekiel 22:30, there is a wall of protection around God's children. But persistent sin breaks down some of the wall and leaves a gap or a breach. When that happens, God looks for someone to "stand before me in the gap." Unfortunately, Ezekiel's generation had no intercessor like Moses and the people were destroyed. Psalm 106:23 refers to what Moses did when Israel made the golden calf: "So he said he would destroy them—had not Moses, his chosen one, stood in the breach before him to keep his wrath from destroying them."

Today, God is looking for those who will stand in the gap as Moses did. You can do that for a person, your church body, or the church at large. Choose a situation and do what Moses did: find out what God thinks about it, reason with Him on the basis of His reputation and glory on earth, and plead on the foundation of His promises.

PERSONAL APPROACH

Create your own prayer for the church using Moses' prayer as an example. Find some specific promises in Scripture you can claim as you pray.

Chapter Thirteen

Learning from Other Prayers

How to Analyze Prayers Yourself

You have just gone through your own study of 12 prayers of Scripture. But there are many more prayers God has provided to mentor us in our own prayer lives. I want to give you a study method that will help you to analyze the remaining prayers of the Bible.

People often ask me how I meditate through the prayers in the Bible. I don't have a formula. For me, however, there are three essential elements in my understanding scripture in general:

Asking for God's help

I take the words of Jesus literally when He said, "The words I have spoken to you are spirit and they are life" (Jn. 6:63). How does one comprehend words that are spirit and life? First Corinthians 2:10 sheds light on this question: "The Spirit searches all things, even the deep things of God."

Because of this truth, the first step for me is to ask God for the help of His Spirit. But, my praying doesn't stop with this initial request. I frequently communicate with the Lord as I work through the prayers in the Bible. I realize the Bible has to be approached with my heart as well as my mind.

Asking the right questions of the passage

I ask lots of questions when going through a prayer in the Bible. Many of these questions are voiced directly to God. Here are some questions I ask:

1. *What is the context of this prayer?* What was happening when the prayer was voiced? This is important. It was this question that helped me understand how profound David's prayer of Psalm 63 was. He was in the desert. That means he was probably running from Saul while he wrote this psalm to God. His life was in great danger, yet he hardly mentioned his own needs.

2. *What did the praying person believe about God that motivated or encouraged him or her to pray the way he or she did?* How did he or she address God? What did he or she say about God? What did he or she believe God could do? To me, this is the most important question to ask of a prayer in the Bible. A person's concept of God dictates when, why, how, and what he or she prays. If you can grasp what the pray-er believed about God, you will be able to get to the heart of his or her prayer. If you believe in a God who exists primarily to give you what you want or need, your prayers will reflect this. The bigger God is to you, the more diverse your praying will be. If you tend to pray the same as you did five years ago, your knowledge of God is probably not growing.

3. *How did the prayer develop?* What did the pray-er first say to God? What were the main thoughts communicated to God? At what point did he or she request action from God? This kind of questioning helped me see prayer in a much broader dimension than just asking God to do something. In Acts 4:24-30 the disciples prayed during a time of crisis, but they spent a lot of time recalling God's sovereign action in history. This type of praying brought them to an unusual conclusion of what to ask of God.

4. *What did the pray-er ask God to do?* This question needs to be asked in the context of the circumstances. There are some prayers in the Bible where people were in great need, yet asked nothing of God. It is interesting to see that Nehemiah prayed 11 times throughout his book, but it is not recorded that he ever asked God to help him build the wall even though that was his major project. Again, in Acts 4 when the lives of the disciples were threatened, they did not ask for

protection. And, when Peter was being harassed by Satan, Jesus simply asked that Peter's faith would not fail. This question is most helpful in that it can help us develop different patterns of asking. We need to be careful not to ask something just because it came to mind or because it is a popular request.

These are the four questions I ask of every prayer in the Bible. There are other questions that come to mind when I'm meditating on a specific prayer. One question that always comes to mind when looking at a prayer in the Old Testament is: *Would this person pray this way if they had lived after the work of Christ?* David sometimes asked God to kill his enemies, but when Jesus came, Jesus said that we should pray for our enemies. The Lord Jesus changed much of how God is working in the world today. Our prayers need to reflect this. The Old Testament prayers are still very helpful in learning to pray. Use them and see them in light of the finished work of Christ.

Asking others for help

Each of us goes to the Bible with a bias. Our family and culturual backgrounds cause us to look at scripture through a certain grid. Most of us have a set of truths that we like to emphasize and we tend to see scripture as related to those particular truths. God made us so that we would function as inter-dependent beings. We need other people.

When studying scripture encourage your friends to ask you questions and allow them to disagree with you. Some of my most valued friends are those who think differently than I do. They ask questions that I don't ask. Sometimes they are hard on me, but I need them.

The praying people of the Bible can be your life-long mentors. Here is a list of several prayers in the Bible. Try analyzing them in light of the three suggestions I have given in this chapter. May the Lord open your eyes to see insights into the hearts and prayers of those who prayed in the Bible.

Reference of prayer	Topic
Psalm 63	God Plus Nothing Equals Praise
John 17	Co-laboring With God in Prayer
2 Chronicles 14:11	Asa's Prayer for Help

Reference of prayer	Topic
1 Thessalonians 3:10-13	God's Responsibility vs Our Responsibility
Psalm 57	David's Prayer and Our Distress
Ephesians 3:14-21	Praying the Mystery of Christ into People
Daniel 9:4-19	Prayer of Compassion and Repentance
Exodus 2:24-25	Groaning Prayers—When Words Simply Won't Do
Genesis 18:17-33	Reasoning With God in Prayer
2 Kings 19:14-19	A Hezekiah-Like Prayer
Job 40:4-5, 42:2-6	Life-Changing Confrontation with the Almighty
Ephesians 3:16-17	Praying for Life-changing Faith
Judges 6	A Discourse between a Common Man and God
Psalm 88	A Prayer of Despair
Romans 11:33-36	A Doxology
Joshua 7	A Time to Interrupt Prayer
Philippians 1:9-11	Prayer Strategy for Spreading the Gospel
Psalm 86	Desperate Praying
Daniel 4:34-37	A Broken Man's Praise
Habakkuk	Prayer that Changes the Pray-er
2 Thessalonians 1:11-12	Praying for Those Who Suffer
Mark 14:32-42	Gethsemane

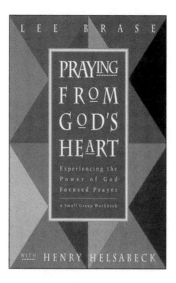

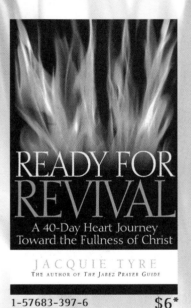

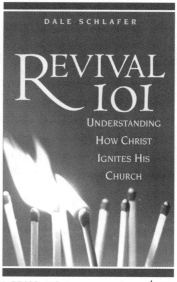